The World
As
I See It

FIRST EDITION

The World As I See It

Poems And Art by

Twyla Hickman

With A Foreword by
Her Friend

COLUMN
GROUP
PRESS

For Ariane, David and Gil

Table Of Contents

BOOK ONE: MY WORLD OF WORDS

BOOK TWO: THE WORLD AS I SEE IT

BOOK THREE: MY WORLD AND ALL THAT I SEE

Introduction

I love the heart of my special friend Twyla Hickman. I know that her poetry reflects her warm and caring personality, her love for Gil her husband, her children and grandchildren, but also I see much evidence in between the lines of her love, faith and devotion to God.

As a retired English teacher, I spent twenty-eight years "trying to teach" the rhyme scheme of an Elizabethan sonnet to high school seniors; I still prefer ordered, organized, rhyming poetry. However, Twyla writes with a stream of consciousness style which expresses her openness, her youth, her fervor, and her desire to share her feelings through the written word. Who says that three quatrains and a concluding couplet are the only way?

Twyla has talent; she loves to write, and I encourage her because I know that writing is cathartic as well as great fun.

Suzi Powers

BOOK ONE

My World Of Words

I dedicate Book One to my son David M. Savoy III and his precious son Jude Michael Savoy. They are the reason, there is hope, and the future is bright for all of us. I had David twenty-seven years ago and was overjoyed at his birth. I heard a voice, saying this child will be the light into the darkness.

Like any mother, my heart became overwhelmed with thankfulness to God. I was so thankful for the child and the blessing that came with him.

Now my son has a son, Jude. He says that this bundle of joy was a great gift of joy and happiness. He said he could never have known what it was like to be a father, if not for Jude.

I hope I can give joy to the world through my poetry. I love writing and sharing my thoughts. Maybe even give hope to others to share their thoughts.

Small Treasures

Waking up on an autumn morn,
Spring showers surprising while working in the yard,
A baby smiling while eating spaghetti,
An elderly person's stories of old.

That special friend's silly mistakes,
Who loves you, no matter what the case may be
That special pet who is always goofing off,
Who also loves you no matter what the case may be.

A rainbow arched three times in the sky.
The smell of fresh cut grass,
Getting a glimpse of a flower opening up,
The smell of fresh baked pies.

A humming bird trying to get nectar,
From a bathing suit hanging on a clothes line,
A squirrel trying to get corn from a feeder,
He decides to get into it, himself.

Jealousy Versus Ambition

Self-ambition is not a blessing.
A person striving for glory,
Never getting the acknowledgement,
It is truly a curse.

Just as jealousy is truly a curse.
It is sad when someone is trying to steal.
A person's name or life,
Jealousy can cause one man to hurt another.

Jealousy may get your self-esteem.
It will cost you your honor.
While you are knocking others, down,
Self-ambition will get you to the top.

Self-ambition is an individual's choice.
Jealousy is an individual's choice.
In comparison what is the difference?
Absolutely nothing can compare.

A Mother's Dream

Many times, she went to the Lord,
She asked for a special person.
Who would make her heart not so hard?
In his infinite wisdom, He sent a perfect person.

Many may say he is larger than life.
Next to her little angel, he stands.
You were to be husband and wife,
In a dream, God told her first hand.

You walked into their lives and it was undoubtedly scary.
Their eyes met for the first time.
It was truly wonderfully eerie,
Remembering the dream of the future time.

His heart is so gentle and easily broken.
He gives himself, without any holds barred.
The love in his eyes is well spoken.
It says it will be steadfast and can never be jarred.

A mother's heart soars with joy at the thought of you.
Holding, cherishing and caring for her little flower.
Blessed by God to have someone like you,
Knowing it is God with His gracious and loving power.

He planned your lives and molded your steps, too.
At the right time when both of you felt lost.
He opened the door and you both knew.
You both would fight to be with one another whatever the cost.

Praying for the day that you two will be one,
Hoping your days together are truly blessed,
With all the joys and hopes and fear for none,
You know the rest.

Twyla Hickman

6

Honor To Stay

Remembering the first time always,
Hoping never to see the last,
Thoughts of joyful days,
Yearning for moments in the past,

With time come memories,
Lasting forever and a day,
Everyday life holds stories.
That gives one a reason to stay.

Art by Twyla Hickman

Crying

Crying sets the soul free.
Crying helps one cope.
It lets the body see.
There is relief and hope.

Why is crying a natural thing?
We can do it for different emotions.
One will even cry if their ears ring.
Crying can seem like an evil potion.

When crying seems rough,
To the body it seems wimp,
If one cries long enough,
The body relaxes and grows limp.

God of Men

God so loved the world,
That he gave his only begotten son,
These are words of great love.
For those who fought evil and won.

Dear God make us worthy, we pray.
Make us like Thee, oh dear Lord.
To honor You every day,
In every way, our Lord.

When we become men of God,
Our lives become an open book.
For God to shape us with His loving rod,
Breaking and shaping us for a new Christian look.

Only A Woman's Pain

Why in a woman's darkest hour,
Sometimes just before the dawn,
In the wee hours of her life,
There seems to be no one.
She can reach out for to give her strength.

You say she is not right with her maker.
Even the seemingly perfect woman,
In every ones eyes,
Feels lost and hopeless at one time or other,
She has that deep dark place.

That place that overwhelms her,
That has been there as a child.
There now as a woman,
The place that her heart cries,
Please! Please! Help me—someone!

It is that silent prayer.
That silent cry for help,
That silent thought is there someone,
Or something that I can do,
To get me through this time once more.

Picture of Love

She is a picture of love.
She is the image of earthly wisdom.
She has gained it through life's rough knocks.
She is precious in His light.

Praying often in silence,
God you have been there.
For her in her trials,
You have been there when she was alone.

She has been a shoulder for others in your eyes.
As a child when others would have folded,
She amazed mere other mortals.
You glorified her empty hours.

She has been down world's lonely roads.
She has made mistakes along the way.
You must have smiled down at her.
She is your unsung hero.

She may be small and even fragile.
In the world's eyes of physical portrayal,
She has someone no one knows.
Her entire strength from You, everyday she shows.

Man Versus Woman

What is the essence of a man?
How is he different from a woman?
A man needs honor and glory.
A woman needs love and to be cherished.

A man can hold his head up,
Only if he feels the right is earned,
He needs that praise,
For a job is well done.

If she would only praise him,
He would walk a thousand miles.
If she would only say how great, he is,
He would climb that mountain.

His only hope is in the reward,
For a job well done,
Telling him of her approving honor and glory,
It comes from her smiling eyes.

Woman Versus Man

What is the essence of a woman?
How is she different from a man?
A woman needs love and to be cherished.
A man needs honor and glory.

She can only blossom,
If he shows her his deepest love,
She can only grow and glow,
If he shows her, his reason for living is she.

She needs his look of approval.
That she is his only love,
She needs his love.
She needs it every minute of every day.

Her hope is in the reward,
For a job well done,
The look in his eyes of love,
She truly is his one and only.

Dear God

He said to her today.
I would give my life,
To cure your pain,
Dear God, I wished it would end.

It is not a mystery.
It is a blessing from God on high.
To those who pray,
Dear God, wishing it would end.

He watches her cry.
He feels so helpless.
Dear God, she cries.
Dear God, wishing it would end.

Now this man stands,
An empty man,
Feelings of helplessness on his heart,
Dear God, wishing it would end.

He lies beside her.
Only heaven knows.
Dear God, they cried.
Dear God, wishing it would end.

Twyla Hickman

The Answer

This is the answer.
Brothers and sisters that you have waited for,
In your moment of despair,
Someone shares your pain.
They have grown to know your secret.

Open your heart's desire to Him.
Even that ever so small of hope,
Your burden will and can be lifted.
He answers the smallest of prayers.
Only if you pray for hope.

Remember, you are not alone.
He knows your deepest darkest secret.
If you do not think, He does.
Call Him and He will answer.
He loves you and that is no joke.

The old saying "been there, done that",
Is not only true for you,
You are not alone you share that pain.
You are truly not alone.
Believe and it is given.

A Gift Of Love

This is a gift of love,
From our family to yours,
The purpose of this gift is,
For the prayers you lifted up in our behalf.

You are the neighbors, we are proud to call friends.
You and your family and friends helped us.
In times, we feared life's ends,
From our bodily ailments.

What is a friend?
The definition says:
One that is well known,
One that which is fond of,

We admit we may not know you well.
We are still very fond of you.
You are our neighbor and a friend.
One who prays, for us at any given time.

Now is the time for you my friend.
A gift of love in a poem,
To you and how we feel,
God bless you in every way.

Thank You!

Christian

He is a man among men.
He is inquisitive and yet reserved.
Filled with pure love,
For God, his family, and his friends

He speaks with youthful intelligence.
He walks as if his feet are groundless.
He has courageous ability.
He has infectious energy to help.

His smile will light up a room.
His heart is easily hurt.
His love for his family and friends,
Makes him strong against his enemy or foe.

His ability to make you laugh,
Truly is a gift from God.
His heart is so generous and giving,
He shares it without been told.

The Decision

Life as a child,
Thinking there must be more than loneliness,
The pains of growing up did not seem very mild.
Thinking of a family to fill the emptiness

Then marring at an early age,
Filled with hopes of love and happiness,
The thoughts of loneliness were no longer on stage.
The words were love, trust, and respectfulness.

Cooking, cleaning and laboring at every job,
To make ends meet,
Oh dear God, why does ones heart throb?
You think the loneliness is through.

He says sorry for the bruises.
He just does not know why.
Wishing there would not be any excuses,
Only that, he would let go with just a good-bye.

Broken both physically and mentally,
Precious children conceived,
Friends come hinting.
Facts, that which is too horrible to believe.

Waiting, hoping the hurt feelings do not show,
Time passes, still confused, who is to blame?
Your anger now I know.
It is time for her to go.

No longer can the pain she bear.
Treated like a stranger and a foe,
Should one leave, because they feel like dirt?
Yes, it is time to go.

The children must be the concern,
It is no longer a choice.
Dear God help them.
Give the strength to raise ones voice.

Twyla Hickman

Zane

Zane what an unusual name,
It fits this little boy of a man,
Who someday shall be great?
He will be a man with the ability to do great things.

He has a soft-spoken voice.
The ability to make his words count,
With a smile that will melt you,
Even forget the anger you had for him.

He is courageous when it counts.
He is tenderhearted with animals and people.
His love for his brothers,
Is undeniable strong

Do not dare him to do something.
He will try his best to do it.
Do not try to tell him to hate.
He will not do it, just to do it.

Yes, for what it is worth.
My money is on him.
To do great things,
Just give him a chance.

Jude

One cold and winter day,
An angel took on an earthly form.
In his mother's and father's eyes,
He was precious and sweet.

His angel like smile melted all who saw him.
His family smiled.
As they kissed him,
They were overwhelmed with joy in their hearts.

God smiled as they named him.
This name is special to Him.
It carries much weight.
It is great for such a little one to carry.

Jude in the Bible,
Wrote a letter of encouragement,
To the people of Christianity,
Of things, God did not like.

He warned to fight against immortality.
As you, sleep little one,
I will pray for the strength and courage,
You will need to fight God's battles.

Little one, in the days to come,
I am sure you will prove to be mighty.
For the Kingdom of God,
His blessings are upon you.

A Gift Of Thanks

Do not get all teary eyed.
It is just a gift of thanks.
We tried to think,
Of a way to say it just right.

We tried and tried to think,
Of what our hearts wanted to say,
For the prayers given up for us,
In our time of need.

As an offering of love,
That is not short of how great we feel.
We composed these thoughts of gratitude,
For the ones who were so wonderful to pray.

We think, we say thanks.
However, as we write, we realize.
Words do not make up our true feelings.
It is just a dent.

We hope you enjoy these words.
Even though, we can't make them say,
The unforgettable thoughts we have of all of you.
Praise God for all of you!

An Aloe Plant

We send an aloe plant.
A gift of love and thanks,
To a wonderful neighbor and friend,
We will always forever appreciate.

Your prayers for our health,
And our well being,
Have made us very thankful,
We live in a neighborhood of friends.

Friends like you, should be cherished,
Like vintage wine,
Never taken for granted,
Nor be ignored for a long time.

As your neighbor and friend,
We hope you like this gift of love and thankfulness.
Hoping that it grows like our friendship,
Strong and healthy and never-ending.

A Sinner's Hope

In this one's lonely hour,
You can feel the absence.
All that matters, seems so sour.
Without any kind of sense.

You can look in the faces,
Of those who want to be,
More than those in lower places,
Only stay close to the potter's knee.

The waiting comes and goes.
The hoping stays constant.
Man's difficulties He knows.
God can make the soul soar to a greater constant.

Thousands Of Times

A thousand times, he said.
A thousand times, she cried.
A thousand times, he prayed.
A thousand times, she prayed.

A thousand times, they wished for a sign.
A thousand times, they prayed for a cure.
A thousand times, they knew God was there.
A thousand times, they confessed His answer.

A thousand times, they look for answers.
A thousand times, they say we cannot believe.
A thousand times, they fall on their knees.
A thousand times, they find the answers in small places.

A thousand times, the answer was there all the time.
A thousand times, the way was right in front of them.
A thousand times, the truest love was there for the asking.
A thousand times, the only one they needed was God.

Twyla Hickman

A Lonesome Cowboy

Once a lonesome cowboy riding a mountain ridge,
Looked down in the valley,
He saw a young woman standing in a field.
The sun captured her figure in her thin cotton dress.

He smiled, as he got closer.
Rubbing her forehead, she looked up.
They found themselves smiling at each other.
She asked if he would like a drink for his horse and him.

He answered shyly, yes.
If it would be no problem,
She smiled and said,
God gave it without a problem.

As the sun was setting,
He thanked her for the cool water.
She thanked him for the friendly conservation.
They walked to his horse without another word.

He got on his horse,
He gave her his cowboy smile.
She smiled back girlishly.
There was a sad parting of two lonely souls.

Grandma said lowly,
That is enough of that same old story.
You must get tired of hearing that story.
About your grandpaw and me

Smiling girlishly, I answered, "never".

A Child Cries

There is a sad time in the world.
When a child cries,
No one hears or listens.
It is the loneliest moment.

God must be so very patient.
When he sees the beginning,
And the end of this pain,
God can only know.

Praying and praising You, God,
Forgive these little ones.
Give the strength to forgive them,
For they are so forgiven.

The love these little ones,
Have for their enemies,
Whether family or foe,
Simply amazes one.

God if only as adults,
We could keep this innocence.
Our life would be so wonderful.
Our love would truly be unconditional.

As A Child

As a child, one does not know.
How to reason out good or bad,
Hearing stories from the Bible,
About good and bad people.

Taught, that one should not hate,
To forgive the sinner,
That includes self,
To pray for the strength to be good.

Childishly, feeling sorry for the devil,
Maybe even praying for him to change,
As an adult, one realizing.
He was the start of evil itself.

As they become adults having children,
Teaching them about good and evil.
Showing examples of good and bad decisions in the Bible,
Showing examples of good and bad decisions, they make in life.

Hoping for their sakes,
That ones teachings are from God.
Bless the little ones,
Moreover, bless the teachers they have.

Cell Phones

The world is changing.
Everything is electric or mechanical.
Everyone has computers or cell phones.
One might think they cannot live without them.

Centuries ago, we would yell to one another.
Years ago, we would call on the phone to one another.
Now days, we type messages to one another.
Wonder what the future holds for one another.

Cell phones are in the home.
Cell phones are in the car.
Cell phones are in the work place.
Cell phones are even in the bathroom.

Looking around at the cell phones,
That are growing out of everyones' ears,
It is no wonder we cannot hear each other.
Because of cell phones, we are talking to our ears.

Circles

Circles have no end.
Circles make life complete.
The word circle has a ring to it.
Circle means a group of things bound together.

There is a circle of friends.
There is a circle of light.
There is a circle of hope.
There is a circle of love.

Circle also means never ending.
It starts with a person,
Ends with another person,
These circles of people make up a group.

A group becomes a family.
A family becomes a part of a friend.
A friend becomes a neighbor.
A neighborhood becomes a community.

A community becomes a village.
A village becomes a town.
A town becomes a city.
A city becomes a county or parish.

A county or parish becomes a state.
A state becomes a nation.
A nation becomes a country.
A country becomes a world.

A world becomes a universe.
A universe becomes a galaxy.
A galaxy becomes infinity.
That becomes God's domain.

The Physician

There are doctors and there are doctors.
What does it take to be a doctor really?
A person of compassion,
For all living things.

His main goal or drive is unfaltering.
It is, without a doubt, self-sacrificing.
To be a doctor is a blessing,
Both for the giver and the receiver.

Countless hours of giving,
Countless days of sacrificing,
Not one hour of work spent idle.
He gives so much to the world.

The world owes him thanks.
Thanks that he must answer to God.
For the privilege and honor,
He has given him a wonderful blessing.

It must be both enlightening,
At the same time saddening,
He finds God has directed his hands,
If he is obedient, God will bless him always.

Life's goal for him is steadfast.
He walks a path of healing.
Even though at times, he may want to cry.
Nevertheless, he recalls, he is only human.

I Love You Little Angel

She said these words often.
She said these words throughout their lives.
She said these words before she left.
She said these words at times of joy.

Most of all, she said them late at night.
If there was a response,
She knew her little ones,
They were awake and not asleep.

Words given,
Either for her benefit or theirs,
These words help in times of despair.
They help to encourage them.

These five little words,
These words of deep love and devotion,
Never giving without thought,
They were words not given lightly.

Bridges

There are many reasons for building a bridge,
Some to connect minds,
Some to connect worlds,
Some to connect time.

Some to connect places,
Some to connect lands,
Some to connect people,
Some to connect lives

There are reasons for these connections.
They make things come together.
They have an awesome effect.
On the things, they unite.

The structure of bridges,
Whether, it is physical or spiritual.
It makes a difference in life.
So much so, those things are never the same.

The bridge between parent and child,
It is so wonderful.
Adults and children,
Bridge together, to become a family.

The bridge between man and God,
Above all, it is the most awesome.
Humans united under God.
They become a spiritual family.

Races

God created us in His own image.
Therefore each one of us,
Is responsible for self,
To act and speak in His likeness

Many say we are the chosen ones.
Whether they are an American or some other race,
Said by each race in defense,
Of each race as the supreme one.

Brothers, we are fools,
If we think this,
God said to love each other,
As you would your own self.

How can we hate each other?
We are truly one race.
The human race,
God is the spiritual leader of that race.

We All Fall Short

We fall short of each other's expectations.
We fall short of each other's hopes.
We fall short of each other's dreams.
We fall short of each other's love.

We fall short of each other's trust.
We fall short of each other's sufferings.
We fall short of each other's accomplishments.
We fall short of each other's truths.

He loves us always.
No matter how much we fall short.
He cares for us always,
No matter how much we fall short.

He blesses us always.
No matter how much we fall short.
He commands that we do the same.
No matter how much we fall short.

Monic

There have been women.
There have been ladies.
However, none compares.
To a lady named Monic.

She walks with lady-like pride.
She talks with assurance.
Her heart gives her away.
Her actions let you know she cares in every way.

If her day is going all wrong,
You will never know it.
If you hurt someone, she loves,
There will be hell to pay.

Knowing her is a blessing in itself.
To call her your friend is an honor,
Hoping she breezes through your life,
If only to share her smile.

God bless this lady.
He always keeps her safe.
She is definitely one of His precious ones.
This unique lady, named Monic.

Time In An Hour Glass

An hourglass counts the time.
Time can be quick or slow.
Watching, time makes it go even slower.
Hoping it would be still only makes it rush.

Time can be deadly.
On the other hand, it can be sweet.
It can even be bittersweet.
Never will it wait.

Time causes things to grow old.
Time causes things to die.
Time causes things to be reborn.
Time causes things to change.

Time is ageless.
Time waits for no man.
Time is one man's blessing,
While time is another man's curse.

Time is never controlled.
Time is never measured.
The sands of time are many.
Moreover, God created all of this.

Questions Without Answers

Can you answer these questions?
Why is it, the poor get poorer,
While the rich get richer,
Do you have the answer?

Why is it, that society rewards laziness?
Ignores a person struggling to succeed.
Is it Satan causing this?
On the other hand, is it just man's own weaknesses?

Why do we ignore our neighbor's pain?
Yet, we open our hearts to far away strangers.
Why do we spend oodles of dollars on pleasure?
However, pinch a penny when God calls us to help.

Why can we see other's faults?
Condemn them with an unforgiving heart.
However we never put ourselves on the chopping block,
Confessing our sins out loud.

We pass by each other
Every day of our lives
Never thinking to ask
Is there something we could do?

No, instead we secretly hope
No one would ask for our help
Maybe sparing a dime or two
Not even sharing prayers for me and you.

A Prayer

Children of innocence are born.
Life is cruel at times,
For children brought into this world,
Many children have to face Satan alone.

Their hopes turn into shame,
He takes their desires of self worth,
And turns them into tears of pain,
Gives them feelings forlorn.

When he thinks he has destroyed them,
He goes for the final blow.
Whispering thoughts of shame even suicide,
To finish their hopeless lives.

God is greater than he is.
God sends angels to them.
Sometimes in the form of someone known,
That may have been lost sometime ago.

Someone who had taught them to survive,
Someone who had taught them there is a God,
Someone who loved deeply,
Moreover, cherish memories of them.

Now, this is the message that needs sharing.
Satan can tempt you only in the five senses.
Pray in your mind and not aloud,
God will send angels to protect you.

God is only a whisper away.
He moves to help everyone,
Who calls on His Name?
Pray for whatever your heart desires.

God answers to those who believe.
A mountain can move for you.
That is His promise to all,
We are His children and His creations.

Twyla Hickman

Believing In God

Some people believe God is kind.
Some people believe God is vengeful.
Some people believe God does not exist.
Some people believe God does exist.

The reason we all believe in something,
God gave us that ability.
Freedom of choice,
Freedom to do good or bad

This will blow your mind.
Even when we are bad,
He continues to love us.
Knowing it is our nature to be bad.

He has the whole picture.
From beginning to the end,
Or if you truly believe,
From creation to infinity

Parents are a good example,
Of what God endures for us,
They may find it hard to discipline.
Out of great love they do it, for us.

When a child is bad,
As a parent, you may get angry.
However, you still love that child,
Even if punishment is the rule.

When a child cries out for help,
The parent wants to help.
If the child repeats the act over and over,
The parent decides to ignore or punish the child.

In God's case, He will send a spirit to guide them.
If they ignore this voice of righteousness,
God will pull His spirit from them,
While He allows Satan to deal with them.

An Elderly Couple

Maybe, you have seen an elderly couple.
They are gray headed and wrinkled with age.
There are twinkles in their eyes.
As they gaze at one another without a word.

Thinking they are so old.
What could make them smile so sweet?
Was it the thought of being together all those years;
They were never apart.

They must have had their share of pain.
They must have had their share of tribulation.
They must have had their share of illnesses.
They must have had their share of loss.

Holding each other's hand,
So tenderly, so lovingly,
It is amazing to watch,
This precious pair

They have been a team all these years.
God please take them together.
If they are separated,
The other would not survive.

Airports

Airports are interesting.
Kind of like bridges,
They bring people together.
They take them away.

Airports are places of unique variety.
You can see all kinds of lifestyles.
You can see all kinds of races.
Airports offer opportunities to greet and meet.

Airports save time.
Airports open a gap in life.
Airports give freedom from traveling fatigue.
Airports are an invention of necessity.

State of Mind

Every state offers something.
State of mind,
State of fatigue,
Even the state of despair,

The state of a country,
Is very impressive,
Take for example the state of Texas,
It offers a state of variety.

From horseback riding,
To the shuttle craft orbiting,
Even a moon lit desert ride,
In a canoe or a carriage,

The state of Alaska,
That is a state of beauty.
How awesome, those black and white mountains,
How wondrous they look.

In fact, every state offers.
Its own diversities,
From Maine to Wyoming,
Their differences are the spice of life.

Twyla Hickman

Hours

Hours of loneliness,
Hours of hopelessness,
Hours of praying,
Hours of endless torment,

You are never able to say,
That which is in your heart,
For fear of rejection,
For fear, your love will go unnoticed.

Hours spent deep in meditation.
Of ways to show or say,
What only you want or need,
These things make ones life bearable.

Satisfaction

They do not dance.
They do not kiss.
They do not love.
The way they did years ago.

How does one please another?
How can you please each other?
We change ourselves,
Trying, hoping to please each other.

One touch is all it takes.
They say one look is all it takes.
Can one know what it takes?
To please another truly.

Twyla Hickman
44

Insight Into Marriage

To have and to hold,
For richer or poorer,
To cherish in sickness and in health,
To honor and obey,
Until death, do you part?

These words are just words.
Devotion is just devotion.
However, to love each other this way,
How do the two of you do this?
How do you end up forever?

You pray for God's guidance.
You wait for His loving direction.
He will always be there for you.
Even if at times, you find it hard to ask Him.
You can choose to listen to His word.

The Greatest Pain

What is the greatest pain?
Many may say physical pain.
Many may say mental pain.
The greatest pain is of the heart.

There is no cure.
There is no treatment.
There is no pill to take to ease it.
No one can escape it.

Pain of the heart,
Grows without attention,
It speaks to every part of the body,
Like a cancer without mercy.

Hoping or acting as if it does not hurt.
It does not lessen the hold.
Praying for a solution,
That is the only ultimate cure, we can behold.

Lovers

She sits there alone.
Hoping he will notice her,
She sits there praying.
He will give her just a look.

One day out of the blue,
He says he loves her.
He wants to show her.
If only she would let him.

What he does not say,
Would show her,
What he does,
Would not show her

Taught to obey without questioning, was his heritage.
Taught to fear everything, was hers.
They both want the same thing.
It lies just within them.

Two people very much in love,
Words needed,
To help their love grow,
However, it is not freely given.

Compromises

Compromise is the foundation of life.
We compromise to get what we want.
We compromise to assure happiness.
We compromise to complete our desires.

Is compromising, the answer?
How long can it endure?
If you compromise,
How much will endure for how long?

Compromise of the heart
It is the worst compromise of all.
Compromising for love
It is never worth the cost.

Giving, what you cannot give.
Living what you cannot live.
It ends up sadly without end.
Alone, it was just too compromising.

What Are You Going To Do?

What are you going to do?
What you need to do?
What are you going to say?
What do you need to say?

Finding the strength, to do what you need to do.
Finding the wisdom to do what you need to know.
Finding the love to give what you need to give.
Finding the word to say what you need to say.

You need to do that which God asks.
You need to share that which God teaches.
You need to share that which God loves.
You need to apply that which God demands.

Let us join God's blessings.
Let us share the messages of the Love.
Let us become God's messengers.
Let us find the reason for the Dove!

The Crown Of Jewels

The crown of jewels,
They are for all to see.
The crown of jewels,
They are for all to have.

Sitting in the dark, praying for the light,
Sitting in a crowd, longing for a friend,
Sitting in prayer, feeling His love,
Sitting in joy, knowing Hope is above.

Gifts make one happy,
These gifts are wonderful blessings.
Gifts filled with hope from above,
They are the blessings filled with life.

God never stops giving these gifts to His children.
God never stops, He is never ceasing.
God never stops sharing His love.
God never stops pouring out His blessings.

Hatred

Hatred is the destruction of one's self.
It eats away at one's morals.
It divides one from all that is good.
It assures that evil wins.

Hatred can cause a person to die empty
Without a soul, comforted in the thought
Empty of one's life,
Of the company of family or friends

Hatred divides people and nations.
Hatred wins when there is no love.
Hatred builds confusion.
Hatred is without the thought of peace.

Hatred is a godless place.
There is no comfort from its sting.
Hatred causes one to feel rejected.
It is the coldest feeling one can give.

My World Of Words

Words can cause a person to dream.
Words can cause a person to foresee the future.
Words can cause a person to succeed.
Words can cause a person to lose his head.

Words create a beginning and an end.
Words create earth-shaking news.
Words create damaging actions.
Words create a past, present and future.

Words can reveal a new world.
Words can reveal a faith beyond understanding.
Words can reveal places you have never been.
Words can reveal your innermost thoughts.

Words can draw a picture.
Words can cause you to see things not there.
Words create a view for you to see eye to eye.
Words can bring you closer to others.

Words can express ones feelings.
Words can bring us closer together.
Words make our thoughts clearer.
Words are truly without saying a blessing.

Twyla Hickman

Art by Twyla Hickman

A Tribute To A Precious Little Angel

This is a special thank you to my daughter, Ariane. She was my strength and encouragement through the times in my life that were so very difficult and lonely. If a person is able to be blessed to have a best friend and that person be their daughter, then I feel that person should count his blessings.

I am so blessed!

She was there, when times seemed to be so dark and lonely. She was there, when no one else would – or cared to – help me. My chronic illness has been a great burden on my family. Even when she was a toddler, I felt the strength she gave me from her spirit. I do and will always be so very thankful for her.

Ariane, I love you more than you will ever know. I thank you for being so nosy and for being so honest to tell me; you found out my secret and thank you for encouraging me to write again and for checking my writings. I thank you for the love you have given me through my life as your mother. You will always be my unsung hero and my most precious little angel.

I hope these poems bring you joy, happiness, laughter, and insight into the Lord's blessings, or if only to entertain you. It will be enough.

May God bless you and keep you safe.

Anna

My lost, but not forgotten, friend.
You gave me the true fountain of life.
You gave me water, when I was thirsty.
You gave me a light when it was dark.
You gave me food from God,
When I was hungry.

Do you remember those words?
Now, I can say, what I thought I could never!
I hope good tidings to you and your family,
I know I will see you again!
If you can forgive my absence,
It was truly not my choice.

I did and will always,
Respect your religious beliefs.
Even though time keeps us apart
All my thoughts and prayers,
To you my friend.

Sandy

I have thought many a time,
That we were always friends.
I know our friendship has passed the test of time,
It never ends.

I hope that we will always be there for each other,
No matter what, no matter when, no matter how,
I promise my friendship will be faithful like no other.
I hope never to let you down, this I vow.

When we are old and gray,
We will laugh and cry as we do now.
I give to you, my friendship forever and a day,
That is a long time, oh wow!

I promise always to be there for you,
Even when I think, there is no possible way.
I hope you feel the same as I do.
What do you say?

Friends forever,
Please!

Dayla

My lovely little flower,
That blooms throughout everyone's life.
Please remember I love you,
Nothing can or will ever change that!

Remember Jehovah is love!
He is your protector.
Rely on him for all things.
He will always light your way.

Dayla, please try to stay in touch,
With your sister and brother
Help one another; find what each does best,
Try to encourage one another.

Dayla, I needed so much to have you near,
Continue to love Jehovah, my little flower.
Everywhere you are, I know someone is touched,
With your pure love.

No greater gift could you receive,
Than the love of God, and all that He gives.
Remember my angel, when you are down,
I will be there, beside you, watching, and smiling.

Until paradise I will wait for you,
All my love.

Ariane

To my sweet precious love,
I love you so deeply.
I know sometimes,
It seems so hard for you,
To understand my thoughts for you.

You and I are quite alike.
I know your thoughts of loneliness,
I will be there with you in spirit,
Trying to give you strength anew,
I promise you.

I got the horse for you,
I did not get you the snow cone machine.
What I got you was a car, Ha
I laughed when you gave it, its first crunch.
I know it was not much.

Remember, if there is a time in your life,
When you need some advice,
Your Dad will be there for you,
To give you strength, courage and calmness,
I Promise!

I will see you in paradise, my love.
All my deepest prayers and hopes,

Always.

David Michael

My beloved son, you are like the water,
That sprinkles across my two flowers.
You always remind us,
That you have an undying strength.

Your strength is seen but at times is hidden
If allowed to grow,
You will be their tower,
And their earthly stronghold.

Please try to learn Jehovah's ways...
There are some, that are hard to understand,
Trust that Jehovah will guide you,
Through the truth.

Do not be afraid to try to do what your heart says
It is in the ways of the Lord
The Lord made you in His image,
So rely on His guidance, always.

I nourished you from my breast.
I felt your need to be ruler or lord over yourself.
Remember, God can help you,
To be just, righteous, courageous and discerning.

All my $50.00,
All God can count,
Love.

Gil

My beloved, should you find this,
If I could live for eternity,
I would want to be with you!
I know I have said that before,
You will just never know.

You once held me in your arms.
Said what no other man has ever said to me,
"I want to make you happy,
Make you forget your pain, if it is in my power,
I want to love your children as my own."

You did just that; be proud my love,
Even if you think, it did not happen.
You did! Much more than you will ever know.
If it did not meet your expectations,
It did mine.

You often saw my tears,
You asked me why I was crying.
"No reason," was the answer so many times.
How foolish of me not to say the truth…
Because I was so happy

I was afraid,
Satan would take it all away!
Please forgive me, for not saying it!
I hope my love was enough for you.
Until eternity, I will wait for you, my love!

Always.

Paw Paw

Once many years ago,
I met my husband's father, for the first time.
A quiet and proper gentle man, I have come to know.
He is very solemn, and tight with a dime!

He is a man of great integrity,
Not easily angered, that is for sure!
His love, for grandmother, is one of deep and loving sincerity,
For he knew long ago, she would always need him a little more!

He can make you laugh, with his dry wit.
You must not take him lightly,
He knows when to fight and when just to sit.
He is an honorable man; I must say quite proudly,

Time has taken its toll,
With his slightly thinning gray hair
He still has a lot of get up and go,
Always a running and going, here and there

When he was young, he worked all the time!
Now that he's retired and at home,
Wishing he could recall the past time!
Now, others go to work and he is at home!"

He's one of the few men, one should truly admire.
He has character that few may never know.
He has lived his life as it always does require,
Never faltering, nor putting on a show!

It is funny how time can slip away.
First, it's not fast, in your youthful days,
Then it starts racing when you're old and gray.
Time hasn't changed Paw Paw though... what can I say!

Let's raise our cups to you saying quite sadly.
God keep you close to Him.
God gave us a friend whom we will miss quite badly
Your earthly light may flicker quite dim.

The light from above we know you saw that day.
Sleep well precious friend, good-bye.
We hope to see you someday.
For now, we will cherish your memories of days gone by.

Your son is your most precious gift to us,
In him, we see your ways, which we all cherish.
Your thoughts are with us,
Our love for you will never perish.

My Cherokee Grandfather

I remember the old Cherokee grandfather of mine,
He was stern and yet gentle... people would say.
As the years rolled around, he just got better like wine.
He was 60 some years young, when he passed away.

He had piercing steel gray eyes, as I recall,
That could see right through you.
His hair once dark brown, was slightly faded and a little bald,
Still he was handsome and somewhat grand, too.

His yes was always yes,
Not many put it to the test.
His no always no, you did not have to guess.
He always tried to do his very best.

His heart was made of gold.
His wife was his greatest love,
But the reason, he always had an empty billfold;
His family and friends were his second love.

He said many times, "You must give the Lord, His due.
It's not what a man says that matters, in life.
It's what he does or doesn't do,
That's what gets him; eternal life."

When he died, the town streets, laden with people he knew,
People honoring this generous man they knew.
I was only six, but even I knew,
The world had lost a great and kind man, too!

Twyla Hickman
64

Ashley

A is for the adorable way; she lets you know she cares.

S is for her shy way of greeting someone new.

H is for her sincere honesty, whenever asked her view.

L is for the loyalty, that she graciously and eagerly gives.

E is for her eagerness to please the Lord.

Y is for her youthful innocence; everyone sees.

My Ashley is definitely unique,

And so wonderfully meek

God bless her in every way,

As she grows in His Love everyday

Gary

I would like to share this between you and me.
I would like to let you know,
What the word BROTHER calls one to be,
From the moment they became a brother you know.
B
Is for the way he seems to be the bravest male,
That is since your dad.
Always like a knight in shining armor, without fail
Not one dares to make someone sad or mad.
R
Is for the way he so fondly wins your respect,
As he masters any and all your problems.
He has an old way of saying, "Oh, what the heck,"
"You just think you have problems!"
O
Is for the open arms,
He always has been there when you need someone to hug.
Gary has always been there with his gentle charms,
Or as the world pulled out from under you the infamous rug
T
Is for the constant trustworthy attitude you see,
When one does rely on him
He has always been there for me,
When no one cared or wanted to go out on a limb.
H
Is for the honest way he answers in his brotherly ways,
All the worldly questions you might have in a day.
He has tried to solve my problems, always,
With sincere honesty but yet in his unique jovial way.
E
Is for everlasting love,
That only a brother can provide.
He has always given his brotherly love,
This helped to withstand the world's ride.
R
Is for the unique relationship of a brother,
That only he can give to anyone.
He is my oldest brother.
Our relationship is very dear and a blessing to one.

Twyla Hickman

Dee

What a fine woman,
She is everyone's idea,
Of what is prim and proper.
She is also one of a kind.

She stands eloquently,
Like a portrait of the Mona Lisa.
Mysterious but so gentle to the eyes,
Her soft voice puts every one at ease.

Could not have stood life's trails,
Without the helping assurance from her,
When nights seem so dim,
She would say just the right thing.

She has uncanny knack for telling it like it is.
Do not think she will not tell you,
If the way you are acting or doing something,
Wrong or not, you had better believe she would.

She is an angel.
Maybe there is no sign of wings.
However, the halo is there,
That is why she's "Miss Wings".

Abigail

On the fourth of July to our delight,
It was our grandchild's birth.
She's God's little angel here on earth.
She possesses this gift from God almighty.

A   is for her unique ability to reason even as a youth.

B   is for the beautiful little angel-like smile.

I   is for her innocence that she boldly expresses.

G   is for the glow she shows in the presence of the Lord.

A   is for the agreeable personality that she possesses.

I   is for her intelligent way of studying things around her.

L   is for the love she shares without hesitation or reservation.

Holidays With The Family

Down at the family homestead,
Thanksgiving or Christmas or New Year's,
There's a lot going on in the kitchen, cause Maw is the Head.
I always get to cut the onions, so I can enjoy a few tears.

You'll never see Maw fixing' her bra. Naw!
Nor Paw a pickin' his teeth,
There's more silliness going on, than you ever saw.
You will never get a sense of grief.

You will never see me acting mean!
I like dogging the football games and yelling!
The boys are a lickin' their plates clean
You know they are content by the size of their bellies, a swellin'!

About midday, it becomes a lazy day,
With paw reclined in his chair,
Maw trying to get help with the dishes, I say!
Everyone out like a light, and you had better beware!

Usually late in the afternoon,
There is always some kind of fight!
Whether you thought, it was a bit too soon,
You'll never see such a sight!

The clan known for cleaning the air,
Paw always a goin' outside,
Maw a saying, "You better beware,"
She's known for, not seeing his side.

By night, Paw's had his 16 little babies,
Maw sure wouldn't have them, I'm sure,
There are no maybes!
The boys just not fit to be a workin' anymore!

Yes! It sure is fun at the old homestead… you bet!
This family is a hoot,
Even if you just met,
They treat everyone like they were a part of their family root.

Love Says Good-Bye

I know this is the hour,
Our hearts are giving a test.
I wish she didn't have to go,
It was not in my power.
As she lays here, her body at rest,
Her soul soars high, I know.

I thought I'd write a last good-bye.
As my story unfolds, to you,
You'll see it's not a farewell!
Even though our hearts may sigh,
This is a tribute to a lady, named Sue.
Who's life was a triumph, that I long to tell.

She often said, "I'm headstrong, yes,
But I'm not stubborn."
Never letting on, she may have felt a bit forlorn,
She would say, "I try to always do my best."
She was not one for blowing her own horn,
Even as far, back, as when she was born.

When you looked at her from worldly views,
Her body held up by crutches.
She may have seemed different, from me and you.
Her legs held together with metal and screws,
Her head held high, like a German Duchess,
You could only see the beauty of this lady, named Sue.

Her days saw no ends,
As she finished her chores,
This could be from cleaning her home
To calling on the sick friends
To the homeless, she never closed her doors,
As though she were always on loan.

Twyla Hickman
70

Her heart went out to the underdog,
While her hands went out to the lost and needy,
And her money to the penniless,
Her mind was sharp, like a captain's log.
It was like doing battle with a skillful lion, not a kitty,
Arguing with her was really quite hopeless!

Her heart was pure as gold,
With thoughts of others,
Constantly giving to family and friends,
Never thinking her body might fold.
Always thinking, ———— they're my brothers!
Never questioning to whom it really depends,

Let's raise our cups to you, Sue, saying farewell, quite sadly!
May God keep you close, to Him.
Life made you my mother-in-law,
God gave us a friend, whom we will miss quite badly,
Your earthly light may flicker quite dim.
The light from above we know that you saw.

Sleep well precious friend, good-bye!
We hope to see you someday,
For now we will cherish,
Your most precious gift, to me, that I cannot deny,
Yes, it's your son, with whom I will always stay.
Our love for you will never perish.

Yeller

Now, that's a faithful name,
It's been pinned on many a feller.
First time, I saw him big and tall with a flaxen tail and mane,
I called him right there... Yeller.
Soon to be known with all his glory and fame,

I got him for my husband to ride,
He, too, is big and tall.
As time would tell, he'd become mine with pride.
I acquired the gentle giant, cause of ailing hoofs, as I recall,
I'd never be the same!

Don't get the idea, that this horse was a registered pedigree!
There was no legal document to see,
To tell of his heritage, I will agree.
He was truly far grander to me,
He was not a bully nor crazy nor loud!

As the days passed and months rolled around,
We all fell in love with that crazy old clown!
His head went up and his stride was abound,
As he strutted in front of store windows, in town;
Getting a glimpse of himself, all shiny and proud!

His intelligence and loyalty surpassed any test.
When we reminiscence about the horses,
We all agree, he was definitely the best,
From all our experiences and sources,
He was the king and the master, too!

On the days, when we would ride,
He would always do something to prove his worth.
Why there was one time, I remember with pride.
A mare, I was breaking, tried to bury me into the earth,
He came a running, and stood over me, until I came to.

Twyla Hickman
72

Even the day he died, proved this mighty giant had unique powers,
You see someone had poisoned him.
He should of have been dead, within twenty four hours,
Even his eyes were so very dim.
The vet said, "Little lady, this horse is fighting just for you!"

He told me, "There's nothing we can do for him, tonight.
You need to take him home,
If he survives 'til morning, he will be all right."
I loaded him up in the trailer, and started for home.
My heart was so heavy, what could I do?

As I turned the last corner for home,
I felt an ungodly jerk, unlike anything I ever felt!
I jumped out and ran to the trailer, and I heard him moan,
Standing with all his strength, as I trembled my heart did melt,
My gentle giant, my knight, my friend,

I reached up and released him from his safety harness,
He took his head and buried it in my chest,
Gently lifted me into the hay with great tenderness,
With a sigh, he laid his head in my lap as if to rest,
"Dear God," I cried, "He's gone, My Friend!"

Bear

I have something that I needed to share.
A story that started with the first time I saw him,
That wonderful dog named Bear.
He came charging at me with excitement and vim!

He was the cutest twenty pounds of fur,
He was only twelve weeks old!
By breeding, they thought he was a cur,
By his markings, he was a Rott proud and bold!

As the months went by, we would come to agree.
It was plain to see, that this dog,
Was one of a kind pedigree.
He did marvelous things like hauling a log.

That is not strange, seeing is believing, guys,
What if then I told you.
The log was three times his size.
He enjoyed the challenge, too.

Once he pinned a guy to the wall,
This pup of six months old,
It was embarrassing, as I recall,
He wouldn't let him move or go.

That may seem strange, I know,
To protect his master, a Rott holds a man,
By his private area and won't let go,
Until his master gives him the cue, that he can.

He would check on the children at night.
Guard them while they played, always in silence,
Like a faithful black knight,
Keeping watch, always willing to put an end to any violence,

Bear was my greatest companion and friend!
In my heart, I can see him rising to follow me,
Even if only to follow me to the den,
His greatest desire was to be with me!

I was so lucky to have known him.
The tricks he did,
Like climbing a tree, not just a limb,
On the other hand, finding whatever I hid.

I taught him the names of different tools,
He could get them for me.
Some friends thought we were just exaggeration fools,
Until he would get the tools for them instead of for me.

Yes, he has gone now, my Bear.
I didn't even get to say good-bye to him... life is so cruel!
He died while I wasn't there!
They said he was play fighting with one of his pups, Bull.

I sometimes think of him,
Running, jumping or just lying next to me,
The nicest memory I have of him,
Is that he always gave his total attention to me.

Tuxedo

Once we found an old stray mama cat.
She was about to give birth.
She was ours, sadly only for that,
She left after she gave birth.

Four kittens were born, to our joy.
Now, please take note.
There were three female tabbies and a boy.
The little boy was the one dressed in a tuxedo coat.

We found homes for them all,
All... except the little boy, Tux or Tux ester,
His name, as I recall,
For his curiosity as a feisty youngster,

We never meant to keep a one!
Just to make sure each went to a good home.
An illness caused Tux, the last one,
To be handicapped, and never to roam

Tux dressed for his natural tuxedo picture,
Bonded to my daughter and her to him... I am guessing.
She became his mother and teacher.
Yes! He was truly a blessing!

He soon acquired unnatural ways,
By watching the dogs through his window,
He imitated them in many ways,
Like sitting on his haunches and begging, what a show!

Art by Twyla Hickman

He fetched straws like a dog, you know
He slept cuddled on the legs of his master.
The two were inseparable from the get go.
He would wait and purr only for his master.

He was precious in his own unique way,
Like a king, sitting on his throne like dome.
He perched on the windowsill during the day,
Until his master came home.

Thank You Lord, I praise Thee,
For giving him to her,
Like a little gift from heaven was he!
My little angel had an angel in a tuxedo fur!

Whale Of A Fish

Once I wished I were a fish... a whale!
Just to see how it would be,
I could tell the tale,
How I swam the deep blue sea!

I would swim as whales often do,
Leaping from the ocean's belly below,
Reaching for the heavenly skies, too,
Confident, I was truly the lord of the ocean, you know!

I would like to swim in the ocean or the sea,
With other fish, no matter what their size,
Yes! They would swim and play with me,
On moonlit nights or even at early sunrise

No one to stop me, this great big fish,
Soon I got to thinking... Is this very wise?
I have seen a fish on a dish,
They definitely were smaller for their size.

My Prince In Blue Jeans

I look at him now,
My prince in blue jeans,
It is hard for some, to see how,
It's not by worldly means.
It is hard to put my finger on it,
Nevertheless, of this, I'm sure; he's the king of wit.

He sits there, his eyes twinkling,
As they do at times.
While he tells a joke; a tale, or storytelling,
Or just some funny lines,
A timidly wise and slightly foolish soul;
He keeps me amazed, with his candid hold.

He has taken me to lakes, mountains, and open fields.
Sharing his views, on God's wonderful creations,
Following him isn't easy, in my five-dollar heels,
Just so, I could share in his mediations!
My blue jean prince is my only true love,
You been sent from above.

My wonderful blue jean prince,
You're my king, my lover, my life.
I both honor you and love you, my prince,
It's wonderful to be your wife!
God's wonderful gift of wisdom,
God has blessed me, from his Kingdom.

God bless you.

The Greatest Of Hobos

He stands a very tall, three foot eight.
A man by his own right, not just fate,
Pants torn and three sizes to big,
Shoes raggedy, and socks with colors so dim.
The shirt displays a town's name or a sig.
His hair is always messy, but a beautiful mahogany red.
Oh! What a sight!
Yes! He's the greatest of Hobos!

He hides the pain of hurt and shame,
Hoping to stop the fear that came,
His father doesn't care… the jerk!
His stepmother is sure to hurt him,
While his father is at work,
He cries in his mom's bed,
Where he knows God hears his plight.
Yes! He's the greatest of Hobos!

He says, "It seems like a nightmare,"
As though life is without any care,
"It's my sister, mom and me,
Against the Devil, you see.
Oh! Why are my father and stepmother so cruel?"
My heart pounds; I want to cry for him.
Instead, I say with great assurance, "YOU are a jewel!"
Yes! He's the greatest of Hobos!

Twyla Hickman

You will see that they are the fools.
You will be pronounced righteous, and the greatest of God's tools.
Someday, they will stand before God, too!
They will cry, "Why punish us; what did we do?"
The Lord will say,
"Yes, you do, remember, what you did!
Get out of my face this day.
Yes! He's the greatest of Hobos!

When he cried, you ignored him.
When he asked for help, you made fun of him.
He asked for food and drink, so very low.
Instead, you denied him, saying, NO!
When he or his sisters were sick or cold,
Whether it is May or December,
You ignored them; you are evil and cold.
Yes! He's the greatest of Hobos!"

Stand tall, my little man, you are one of a kind.
Don't worry; you're an attribute to mankind.
Even through all the pain,
Your rewards were an easy gain.
You give your love without hesitation.
You've been so kind.
God smiles, when He hears your mediation.
Yes! He's the greatest of Hobos!

A New-Found Friend

I thank God, for bringing into my life, a friend.
It proves... He is all knowing,
He knew we would be there for each other to the end.
We've become so close without even trying.

We are like two vines, intertwining as we are growing.
Yes, it's quite strange to both you and me,
Your life and mine always are crossing!
Yes, this divine plan meant to be.

Let's keep in constant touch, please!
Our lives together, are truly a blessing.
Our friendship can and will withstand, the roughest seas.
I have a new-found friend, without any questioning.

A Long Lost Friend

My dear friend, I thought of you today,
I said, "I must write her, without delay.
No! I must call her...
No! I must go and see her,
Without deliberation.

As I sat at my desk,
I thought, "It's been a day or two, I guess.
No! It's been a week or two.
No! It's been a month... you fool!
Oh, Lord, it's been a year, without any more hesitation.

I gathered up my purse and bible, from the table,
My eye caught a glimpse of a message... a wireless cable.
It read... "In the presence of only a few,
Our dear friend passed away, today, at St. Lou.
Sorry, for the delay."

The Loneliest Soul

Old shoes stand in the hall,
Like a fireman's, ready for the next call,
Dirty pants on the bathroom floor,
Suggest that he couldn't take another step any more.
A shirt hangs on the chair,
He thinks that there might be one more wear.

His heart is heavy,
With pains, that seems to vary.
It is in his eyes,
It is in his sighs.
This wonderful man with eyes that never cry;
Refusing the unavoidable changes... and won't even try!

A man of strength, and with great pride,
Head held high, but with a little slower stride.
His blue eyes seem a little tidier,
He still has that drive like a prizefighter!
He's still the only man for me,
My love for him you surely can see!

Pray God will relieve his pain, some way.
Knowing the Lord will do it some how, in his infinite way.
Faithfully, giving thanks to the Lord,
Knowing that the Lord is keeping guard,
Like a noble shepherd,
Tending to that one, wandering just a little from His herd.

Thoughts Of Time

SECONDS COUNT DOWN

MINUTES TICK AWAY

HOURS PASS BY

DAYS FLY BY

WEEKS COME AND GO

MONTHS TURN INTO YEARS

YEARS TURN INTO CENTURIES

CENTURIES STAND THE TEST OF TIME

Happy 50th Anniversary

Dear friends and family, it's with great attention,
To pay tribute to a great lady and wonderful man, today,
First, it does well to mention,
They celebrate 50 years of marriage, what does that say.

It's a witness to a lifetime of commitment,
50 years they've been united faithfully,
Knowing what the words, "I DO," really have meant.
Their deep love and trust, comes so naturally.

Always there for each other, like good friends.
Now, he is a hoot, with his mischievous smile.
She is the one who consoles, builds up, and even mends.
United in a perfect style.

He is the strength in her life,
He has a quiet and humble manner and without any rest.
He is the unique head behind your wife.
He is the proof of what it takes to pass the test.

No words can express!
Her overwhelming kindness and sincere love,
She's the reason their marriage is such a success,
That is why God smiles from above.

When you first meet them, one will know,
What love is by their open arms,
She with her loving glow,
He is like a knight full of charms.

Asked, "In a marriage, what is a must?"
He whimsically says, "PATIENCE! And a lot I'd say,"
Some hope and trust,
Letting her have her own way.

She answers in only a few words,
She smiled and said, "Oh, you just find the strength."
Like a cowboy watching over several herds,
For years, you've been the pillar of strength.

So today, we raise our glass,
To both of you, with a marriage of gold,
May your motor home never run out of gas!
God bless you both, as the roads unfold.

Three Things A Person Is Never Able To Take Back

(Words told to me by my biological father and my thoughts on them)

1. A SPENT HOUR
"Good or bad whatever you wanted to do, or say, can never be undone, you have wasted the time to do it."

2. A SPOKEN WORD
"Good or bad whatever you wanted to do or say, can never be, you have wasted the time to do it."

3. A NEGLECTED OPPORTUNITY
"Good or bad whatever you could have done, it can never be done later because you had that one chance to make a difference!)

Life

A bowl of jelly is like life it is told.
You can shape it, like a mold,
To fit your very soul,
Living life to its fullest, my friend,
It can be more rewarding, even to the end...
Than just watching, it unfold.

I for one am very sure,
I would rather not be a rider of a tour.
I would rather be the driver,
Of my vessel on a great quest,
Not knowing, if I would or could rest,
Than a mere observer or rider.

Thoughts

I have a thought!
Do material things in life matter?
As we are so often taught,
Do we run around, like a mad hatter?
Hoping to find something of true value.

It's not around the corner.
It's not in the neighbor's pool.
It's not at the park like Garner.
Not even in a bar on a stool,
Do you want to know?

Three things that is true!
This is all you have to know.
I say quiet simply to you,
"What makes our lives grow?
They are pure love, faith, and trust!

Your love, for God, should be,
Driven like the snow.
Your faith in Him should be,
Strong and shine with a glow.
Knowing He is there, always at our plea.

Trust Him, when He says, "You have no past.
I've slain the beast,
You are free a last!"
Join Him in the feast,
For all eternity's days.

Twyla Hickman

Jealousy

Jealousy is a disease,
A person may think it's pure.
If the one receiving this love, surely is not at ease.
Then that love is not very sure,

Some call it the green-eyed reaper.
Without any thought or question.
It is the old deceiver.
It makes you think... love is possession,

If it, in itself, is bad,
Then why is God, a jealous God?
Remember, we are like our Dad.
Could there be a degree, you should have had?

It's a gift not to control.
A blessing not a cancer,
To give freedom; not to hold,
This is the answer.

To love the one you want to love,
Give your precious one,
Give the one you want your love.
Free reins to be able to run

You are blessed,
By the tearful joy, running down their eye,
As their lips are pressed,
To yours, telling you, "My Love will never die!"

The Hardest Job –
Being A Parent

There comes a time in every parent's life,
When he realizes he doesn't always have the infinite answer,
To all of his child's problems and strife,
The pain and hurt, when a parent fails, is like trying to cure cancer.
It never seems you did all you could,
To cure their pain, like you should.

There's no salary paid,
To fight the confusion and doubts,
That comes with each decision made.
It makes you wish you had taken those different routes.
Being a parent is the hardest job; I know in life;
The rejection at times, cuts like a knife.

It begins with the night shift blues,
After they are born,
Their first steps, should give us our first clues.
We just sit there with our bodies worn,
With the joy in our hearts,
Constantly assured; these little ones will have better starts.

When they're little children,
They walk all over our feet.
When they're older, they walk all over our heart, my friend.
Never thinking, someday that they'll be in this seat.
A father, mother, or guardian to someone,
Taking responsibility for their child's choices, as they have done

I chose to be a parent, myself, long time ago,
My husband chose to be a guardian to my children.
Through the years, we've felt that sometimes we were their foe.
Neither a parent, nor a leader, or a friend,
If we had to do it all again,
You bet, we would, even after all the pain.

Twyla Hickman
92

Things I Know

The saddest thing, in life, to know,
Some may never know!
They don't have to prove their worth,
It was theirs at birth!

The loneliest thing in life, to see,
Some may never see,
They have a person, who loves them,
No matter if, the light seems dim to them.

The cruelest thing in life, to know,
Is that some are blinded, and know not where to go.
Satan used his bag of evil tricks,
To keep them from seeing, through his evil wall of bricks.

The greatest love and hope, to know,
Is for all to share God's eternal show
All He wants for us is... forever!
Live in happiness, and peace and not fearing ever!

The Hardest Thing To Do

You know Lord; it was the hardest thing to do!
Looking into their eyes, and seeing the fear and tears,
"We're hungry mamma!" What could you do?
"Oh! Mama" they cried, "he promised us more, all these years."

You know Lord; it was the hardest thing to do!
A woman beaten; a mother alone,
Giving up hope if only it were not you,
You stand, watch, and think and silently moan.

You thought they would be protected, loved, and helped to grow?
Like a knife cutting into your soul, too?
You give them up for all the wrong reasons, how could you know?
Lord, it was the hardest thing to do!

You pray day and night, "Help you get them back, please!
PLEASE, just one more chance for you to love,"
You would never give them up, you'll see!
You would teach them to love.

Until then, you stand at a distance, praying, loving, and hoping.
You remember; Lord, you are coping.
It was the hardest thing you ever did in your life!
It was the hardest thing you have ever done in your life!

Twyla Hickman
94

Why?

Why is a man so weak?
He says he's strong and true,
Then turns to you, so meek,
It's true they all soon glorify you.

As women will cry out, in labor pain,
First, for their husbands, then their mothers,
Even the atheist will call your name, in vain,
In the final hour, above all others

I witness many things, from God, in awe.
A small child abandoned.
A man unable to work within the law,
Or a woman stranded.

God, you are Lord Almighty,
So why does man continue to deny you?
Satan is doomed (all neat and tidy),
With a future without a view

With Jesus, as your king, of this world,
There's nothing to deny.
Let your sovereignty unfurl.
Glory is to the King on high!

He

I thought of life and its many troubles.
Just as I thought, it was over,
You made me laugh, and it was only the beginning.
Yes, I owe you a lot ... And then some more.

Maybe more than anyone may know,
Because God gave you, to me,
In His Wisdom.
You're the first thing I think of in the morning.

After God hears my prayers,
As the poets say, so charmingly,
"The last thing at night"
I ask God to give me strength.

And to give me hope,
He gives me a holy light,
That lights up my weakest hope.
Only He knows what I need.

God, you gave me a strong and loving spouse.
God, your light helps me.
You are the source of my energy,
And the center of my life.

Twyla Hickman

Do You Know?

Often, we are told
"Life must go on, you know."
Like the ticking of time,
Life's heart beats, yours and mine.
Then why the forbidden coffin,
No! Jesus loves me, this I know!
You ask me, "How is it that you know?"

'Cause I see it when a baby cries,
Deep into their eyes,
I see it, when the unsung hero's eyes
Reach out and search the skies.
In despair, many search the lies!
God whispers, "Here's my son!
For you on earth, to save not just one."

He saves all from the lies,
Some say He just isn't so.
Who receives the savior's gift, you know?
Quenches the spirit's thirst,
Who will be the first?
"Forgive me," before he dies,
Life just has to go on, you know.

No! Jesus loves you, this I know.
Jesus never thought that we were nothing.
My Jesus gave me everything.
He gave His life, His soul for me, now that's something!
More precious than you will ever know!
'Cause Jesus loves us, this I know.
Now, you can say, "Do you know?"

A Woman's Heart

A woman's heart is to me,
God's most precious thought.
He gave her that to play the part for Thee,
She could be the help he sought.
Man could be the head,
From the kiss at the time, they wed.

Her heart is just like cotton candy,
A touch of spring water,
The sweet taste of steadfast love is quite handy!
The strength of a selfless mortar,
Mixed with the constant flow of a concerned mother,
The Master's work is in her, like no other.

Her heart sends a flow of thoughts, to her Lord!
He lets her know, her work is never done.
It's always saying with this love, it's never hard.
She's the Lord's unselfish one!
Man's strength comes from above,
A woman's strength comes from her heart with love!

Yes, the heart of a woman,
Is the foundation of love and tenderness?
She will strengthen and encourage her man,
Against the odds, filled with hopelessness,
It gives the one she loves, hope to stand.
God in His awesome plan,

He has always meant for her,
To have and hold only one man, you know,
He would truly be complete with her.
So next time you think; she's losing her glow,
Remember the man in her life is the only one,
Who can keep the love in her heart won!

A Woman's Love

As I sit and think about you,
I try to say what's in a woman's heart.
I try to say what poets, only wish they knew...
A woman's love... And where should I start?

I try to say, "I love you," a thousand times,
Just saying the words is pointless.
I try to show you the ways, I love you, often times,
It's just a snapshot, of the greatest love... nonetheless!

God made man, which started the master's plan,
A woman from the first man, as His love token,
They say that was the first love relation of man.
I LOVE YOU (the greatest words ever spoken).

If I had but one thing to give you,
I would give you this... My love.
My love pure, and totally yours, too
For you to share that love with God, above.

Because He sent me to you from above,
With a sign so you would know,
He gave me to you with His love.
United with Him, as pure as snow.

I Wish I Could Say – Love

My love, I wish I could say love.
I wish I could say what I mean,
So what I mean, could be said, my love.
Do you know what I mean?

I want love and to be loved,
If my love could be your love,
We'd be each, others… Beloved.
Then I know I'd be your love.

Please open your heart!
I only want you, love!
Hear the songs of my heart.
Will you have my love?

A Woman...
Why Must She Cry?

I give my heart to you,
There is no laughter.
I give my hand to you, my love.
There's no feeling.
Tell me why, must a woman cry.
Tell me why, must she look so sad.

They say a man is afraid to cry,
That a man never forgets his pride,
A man is a fool.
He never gets what he is after.
Tell me why, must a woman cry.
Tell me why, must she look so sad.

A woman can love and forgive,
A man never says I am sorry.
She can love, hate, and laugh,
Most of all she forgives.
Tell me why, must a woman cry.
Tell me why, must she look so sad.

God gives her laughter, happiness, and love,
She's just tired of sadness, loneliness, and pain.
She will give back to the world its property.
Please give her... Back her life!
Tell me why, must a woman cry.
Tell me why, must she look so sad.

A Vessel Of The Lord

Here, I am at forty-eight.
A woman, a mother, and a wife.
What is my life's fate?
At this time in my life,

I think I should just do it,
Whatever the infinite plan would be,
Not worry, whether I am really fit,
Let the Lord lead me.

When I wake up, Lord, You're the one I want to talk to,
When I go to bed or lay down my head,
I want always to remember you.
All my life's many woes, I give up to You, Lord, instead.

Oh! Lord, thank You for being you,
Thank you for loving me,
I will always give my very best too.
In every thing, I shall ever do or be.

Please! Give Me A Little

I asked them, "Please for my sake,
A little time, a little hope, just a little,
Even if at first it may seem fake,
Why can't you just give a little?"

Why does it always seem,
We see things different later.
It becomes so clear, like a dream,
Always like an unwilling traitor.

He asked, "Give me a day, would you?"
"No!" They say! "Well then would you give me an hour?"
"No!" They say! "Then could you spare me a minute or two?"
"No! I'm sorry you don't have it in your power."

I hope you do not wait to long.
I love you, and I know he loves you, too.
I forgive you, because it's not wrong,
To love you every day anew.

Do it for him, please!
Please do not wait on the final hour!
Would you do it, for me?
My heart will hurt, if you lose your spiritual power.

Who Am I?

Am I the person who loves?
Or the one that is loved?
Am I the person who creates?
Or am I the one who enjoys the creation,
Am I the person who gives?
Or the one who receives?

I hope I am the one, who loves,
And gives it freely,
I hope, I am the one, who creates,
In order to glorify my Lord deeply,
I hope I am the one, who gives,
In order for my Lord, to be amplified more sincerely.

I know how and why I love,
I do not know where it will go.
I know I love to create things,
Which is a gift from above, you know.
I know I am a giver of joy,
Which I have come to know.

All my love, abilities, and offerings,
Are only as joyful and complete,
As my constant prayer for a holy gathering,
To glorify Him with my spiritual pleat,
It becomes abundantly clear.
Who I am and why I am so dear.

Twyla Hickman

Faithful Throughout

As she lay there in pain,
Her small body curled up.
She cries out in vain.
Is there not one who will fill her cup?

She prays for mercy, first!
She hopes for salvation.
She cries for water to quench her thirst,
She waits for the holy justification.

God please give her that holy touch!
She will know your wonderful love.
She will feel your glorious clutch,
Finally, know you are above.

You will remember her faithfulness,
Oh, Lord almighty, proudly,
She never waivers under Satan's evilness,
She gives you the glory, loudly!

I pray her soul to rest one day,
In Your mighty Kingdom,
For she is your servant in every way,
Now, grant her the greatest peace to come!

The Lord's Faithful Servant

Lord, I tried so hard but failed,
To tell them of your wonderful powers,
How do you tell a fool who's jailed,
In a cage with the Devil, and his followers?

He has told them lies for so long,
Their eyes and ears closed to them.
They do not think that they belong.
They do not think Your Son rose from the dead to save them.

My heart… My very soul cries,
For my brothers whose hope they've lost!
How can they forget the day Your Son did rise?
He paid the cost!

God grant me an unquenchable thirst,
To spread the Word,
That each one of us can be the first,
To hear Your Holy Spirit and soar like a bird!

Twyla Hickman

I Believe In Angels

I sit here quietly thinking,
Do I believe in angels?
"Why yes," I say without even blinking.
They are all around us these angels.

They watch us struggling to withstand Satan's hold.
I believe they stand in awe at our God fearing trust,
(We creatures of this earthly fold)
As we sometimes rejoice or when we even, bite the dust.

They walk with us in our daily ways,
Observing, how we deal with our choices.
Even at times, they help us overcome what evil says,
These beautiful creatures with their heavenly voices.

You may ask, "What does it matter?
Because I saw one when I was young,
It stopped me before I climbed my life's ladder,
With the noose around my neck to be hung.

So sweet angels of God, almighty,
I thank you for the love on high.
As I go to sleep, I will cherish His love, nightly,
Bid you, my angels, ado, and not good-bye!

Christmas — Bah Humbug!

I hate the fact that people say,
It's the most joyful time of the year.
I hate that they say, "It's the Lord's day,"
Laugh, joke, and drink beer.

I hate the way people rush around town,
Spreading joy and good tiding,
Forgetting there is so many down,
With no place, or someone that would be inviting.

Would it not be nice?
If we would rush around all year and every day,
Opening our doors to all, without thinking twice,
Hoping to show an image of the Lord in what we do and say.

Twyla Hickman

The Voice of God

Lord, I know you are always present,
Many may never want to know.
I hear your voice, which you sent,
To help me make the right choice where to go.

If I could help but one lost soul,
To learn to hear your voice,
Then they, too, would learn our earthly goal,
Hear your voice to make the choice.

It's sad to me,
To think some even lose the right,
To hear the loving voice of Thee,
They stand alone, poor fools, against Satan to fight!

Then their guilt they feel no more,
Your voice becomes less and less.
Until finally, there is a closing to life's door,
Your voice is gone forever more!

My Savior God To Thee

I stand before my earthly family,
To be judged, if I'm pure and holy.
I do not mind their rejection completely,
Lord; please help me, my King, Most Holy.

Lord, I know I'm not perfect, to any ones surprise,
With Your Guidance and Love,
I will survive, and I will rise,
To complete the task you have given me from above.

Give me the strength my enemy to face.
I do not ask for worldly riches.
I just want to know your awesome grace,
Be able to tell how you have helped fulfill all my wishes!

You have always, and forever will be there!
Only, it's so hard Father,
To see the pain they have to bear.
'Cause of ignorance, they won't help their brother.

I promise to stand faithful through it all.
Your Holy Spirit, surely, will guide me.
I will be successful in breaking Satan's wall,
I will give the glory, my God to thee!

Twyla Hickman

The World As I See It

They say time is just a measure of life.
I say it is just the vision of the Lord.
They say happiness is just a measure of man's thoughts.
I say it's just the love of the Lord.

They say money is the root of evil.
I say its man way to rule over one another.
They say money can't buy you happiness.
I say happiness doesn't need money.

They say there is no God.
I say it takes a fool to say there is no God.
They say evolution created the world.
I say revelation created the world.

They say there was no Jesus.
I say there was a man that died for all humankind.
They say there is no hope for humankind.
I say humankind is not hopeless, just slightly misinformed.

They say there are not anymore good and honest people.
I say it is hard to be good and honest, but we can be.
They say there is prejudice in this world.
I say there are uneducated people to God's laws.

They say marriage is like a ball and chain.
I say marriage is God's greatest creation, this union.
They say it's a man's world.
I say it's God's holy creation.

They say we're living in the last days.
I say we are living in the last hours.
They say when you die you may come back as some kind of animal;
I say that when you die you answer for your life as you lived it.

Art by Twyla Hickman

BOOK THREE

My World
And All That I See

I dedicate this book to my friend and neighbor Suzie Powers. She is a retired schoolteacher, but she took the time to read my poetry and gave me the encouragement I needed. We have only been neighbors for a couple of years. However, our friendship will pass the test of time. She is an absolute jewel of God. When he created her, he must have said, "And that is good!"

She has an aura about her, that when you are in her presence, you just have to be happy. She has a way of saying things to a person that makes them want to be a better person. Like that twinkle in her eyes when she is poking fun at her wonderful and one of a kind husband, Sam.

I just hope God will allow me to have many more days and hours to share with her. She has given me so much encouragement that I cannot begin to thank her enough.

Suzie if you read this, remember I love you very much. I thank you for your infinite wisdom, guidance, love and friendship.

Twyla

He's There For You and Me

We run around like chickens,
Looking for a place to roost,
Not knowing where the road bends,
If you'll get a blessed boost,
There is no telling.
What they are really selling.

They give you tickets free,
To shows of magic and trickery,
To plays about a daring deed for you to see,
Or an opera about some tragedy,
So few come to know the joy,
Of the awesome Lord, who once was a boy?

He grew into a young man, quite noble,
Died before his time,
The only story told was that of the Bible,
Of this awesome Lord of mine,
I want to share his life and words with you,
So you, too, can have some hope of a holy view.

Twyla Hickman
114

Don't Take God For Granted

I look at you and want to say...
Please do not take life's blessings for granted.
I know if I do, you will just say, "It doesn't pay to pray"
Go on acting as if nothing is important.

What I have to say is very important!
"If you don't treasure each and every moment,
Thank God for what he has felt to grant,
God will take his gift from you, in one quick moment."

Don't think that you are the one and only,
There was someone before you.
You ask for the blessing to be yours truly,
Beware... there can be someone after you!

Heed my words and take them to heart,
"God gave you a blessing,
He wants you to treasure it and don't pick it apart,
I assure you, He will and can take away the blessing."

Often, you cried for a special someone.
God sends that person to you,
All you can say is, "You don't know what he's done!"
Poor fool; I hope you can stand the lonely view.

Who Are You And I?

As I lie in bed at night.
The world is a sleep.
I feel the thoughts of my worldly fight.
I have needs that I want to keep.

I feel the lord sent you to me.
To watch over me as your wife,
Our children to oversee,
Joyfully is our life.

Satan tried to tear apart our fates.
With lies that sound logical,
Even sensible as responsible mates,
We are sure we are practical.

The lord is merciful always.
He chose us to be intellectual.
We become dependable in a mirror of His ways,
Without becoming cynical

If we watch what our mouths pour forth.
Never letting them become radical,
We can take what You say.
And we can call it factual.

Twyla Hickman

Shadows

Have you ever thought?
What would it be like, if you were only a shadow?
Mere darkness with lights naught,
No movement seen in a window,
Because it's a shadow.

Shadows move quietly.
No feeling or sense of life,
They make things seem quite frightfully,
As though it were cutting like a knife.
Because it's a shadow.

Shadows can make you laugh.
Shadows can make you scream and shutter,
Like a small baby calf,
When he has lost, his mother's utter,
Because it's a shadow.

Shadows are like lost souls.
They only know how to mock.
They follow the ones, who lead the folds,
Never leading the flock,
Because it's a shadow.

I don't think I would like being a shadow,
I like the sunlight on my face.
That's wonderfully warming, you know,
Than being alone in a dark place,
Because it's a shadow.

Secrets That Hurt

When a person keeps a secret,
That's all right because it's his.
If a person tells a secret,
That's a broken promise of his.

I told a friend a secret of my heart.
He told me of his, too.
I tried to help him from the start,
He didn't seem to understand what to do.

I poured out my soul without hesitation.
He shared his most secret dream.
Crying, laughing, most of all; we knew each other's situation.
We were always on each other's team.

We began to depart from each other.
One harsh word thrown into the pan,
To belittle at any cost ones brother.
Who knows how great the pain?

The secret told by a lover or a friend.
It cuts like a knife deep and cold.
There's nothing but empty feelings at the end,
From the secret that is told.

If I have a secret, this is what I'll do.
I'll keep it to myself.
There's no hurt—for me or you.
No one is to blame for the pain, except to ones self.

Twyla Hickman
118

My Love Delights In You

My love is like a racing red car,
It's in overdrive most of the time.
I've tried to keep it in idle or park,
I can go really far!
It just won't gear down every time.
It seems just to need a little spark.

My love delights in his look that comes across the room.
His touch makes my heart skip a beat,
When no one is looking,
It takes a super charge, like a sonic boom,
Every time we meet.
The special delight is that my love is constantly working.

I could give my love to the world,
They could experience my pleasure,
Their hearts would surely know love.
They say the older we become, in this world,
Our delight in each other is obvious that's for sure.
It completes life's grandest love.

My love delights daily,
In the way, he holds me.
When I'm afraid or when he wants to cuddle with me.
Time after time the little smile, ever so slightly,
Saying I told you so or don't you see.
This is only a few of my love's delights, you see!

A Definition of Love

How does one measure love
Some may say,
"How much do you love me?"
Can I share my view with you today!

Love is that well worn ear,
That doesn't ever seem to be tired,
Of listen to one more fear,
Some wish that hasn't transpired.

Love is that dipped shoulder, more than slightly,
From hours of listening to those with seemingly lost hope.
Never reluctant to give its extension openly,
Nor fearing it couldn't cope.

Love is the well-worn knees of its bearer,
Spent praying for a brother's spiritual needs,
Hours spent in prayer,
For the healing love of ones earthly needs.

Love is that face that glows,
When you enter the room,
You know love and have no foes.
You're safe in their arms, neither fear nor gloom.

Twyla Hickman

Flowers

Flowers have many forms of delight.
They give off color and fragrances of many ranges.
They shower the world with color by day and by night,
With their exquisite changes,
Some with their alluring dangers

A flower by its God given name,
May burst forth any minute of the day,
To let you know, it's a flower just the same.
Giving its viewer something to say,
Look at this rare and unusual flower!"

Walking through a field in a valley or up a mountain side,
Gives you the thrill of a flower stage,
Standing at attention with great pride,
One must applaud the range of many types of vintage.
That entertain all ones senses and to rally forth.

Thank You, God, I pray you hear me.
I lie here in awe of your wondrous world.
Your majestic coloring book consumes me,
Everything around me begins to unfurl,
They were thanking you for the gift of life so sweetly.

Stranger

Stranger is a word,
That causes me to ponder.
What makes it seem lonely when heard?
Sad, as through life, I wander.

When you enter a place - a room,
Do you feel at ease with others?
Do you act like the Man in the Moon?
Just a reflection from others.

So lonely with empty tomorrow's,
Not to be able to be a part,
Of someone else's every day joys or sorrows,
Share in secrets of the heart.

A stranger never knows how you feel.
He never knows how or what to do.
A stranger can't forgive, so you can heal,
From angry words or deeds to name a few.

A stranger can't ask for help or hope,
To save his soul,
Nor the distance be removed, so he can cope,
And maybe enter God's heavenly fold.

I believe every one is a stranger,
None of us wants to be.
We need to know the only danger,
Is in not asking, "Can we be friends, you and me?

The Power of the Almighty

Have you ever heard this question?
Whose God is yours?
One made by only mere suggestion?
To soothe our hope, mine and yours.

Look around–I dare you!
Note the miracle of life is His.
Can you see from a Mountain View?
That this creation is made by an awesome whiz.

Man with his marvelous dreams,
Could never imagine with such zeal
For instance, the many springs and streams,
Filled with various fish, by God's own Will.

The power of God almighty is grand.
It gives such joy, hope, and peace to you and me.
He creates with the help of the Holy Spirit's hand.
He's flawless, the God of whom we cannot see!

Marriage Vows

I promise to love you,
With all of life's many offerings,
I promise to love you,
With God's infinite blessings,

I promise to cherish you,
With unshakable support,
I promise to cherish you,
With devotional admiration of a great sort.

I promise to obey you,
I'll try to see your point, my love.
I promise to obey you,
That means I'll always do.

I promise to care for you,
In sickness and in health,
I promise to care for you,
In rags or wealth.

I promise to trust you,
In every aspect of our life,
I promise to trust you,
In all our trails that come in life.

I will always honor you,
For as long as I should live,
I will always honor you,
For as long as it is mine to give.

I will always respect you,
As my marriage partner forever,
I will always respect you,
As a part of myself forever.

I will stand by you,
When things around us seem dim,
I will stand by you,
As we pray for guidance from Him.

You will always be mine,
I will always be yours.
You will always be mine,
As we walk together on Heaven's shores.

A Man Of God

A man of God,
Do you know the qualities of him?
He is humble before God.
Because of his knowledge of Him

He has the wisdom to show love,
Without caring for its return, Lord.
His comfort comes from above.
Displayed in his life's many trials, Lord

This man of God for all to know,
Talks and walks with Him.
God's eternal light in him does show.
Hours of prayer until life's light goes dim.

The glorious hour for this man,
Comes after his job is done.
He'll proudly shout, "Yes, I can."
Without a doubt, he is the one.

Who is this man of God's holy band?
It's you and me.
Yes, if only we will stand,
For what we believe, you and me.

Life's Works

Standing before the Holy throne,
Ones life to testify,
Ones faults to Him be known.
Ones hopes and works testify.

Looking to you, oh Lord,
One cannot justify ones hates,
Nor ones sins in the book, that are stored,
To hope for a chance at Heaven's gates.

Standing there with bloodguilt, Oh, Lord,
Ones own sorrows of earthly pain,
How does one thank You, Oh, Lord.
With this entire spiritual bloodstain.

Oh, Jesus, Please forgive thee!
Knowing one does not come close to Thee,
However, the joy in Jesus, one knows and can see.
Seeking the place of the righteous Lamb of Thee.

The final hour of ones earthly life,
Will be a glorious one,
To have fought the great battle of life,
Moreover, knowing you have won.

God The Father

I feel safe with you,
In the darkest times,
I feel safe with you,
In the loneliest times.

You give me hope,
In the trials of this world,
You give me hope,
Every time Satan's darts do unfurl.

There's no greater love,
That I've ever known.
There's no greater love,
Than God Almighty's, own.

If I could share Your love,
With those who know You not, I pray.
If I could share Your love,
There would be no lonely fools, today.

Thank You, Father God,
For the love, You share with me.
Thank You, Father God,
For the comfort and joy, I see.

Twyla Hickman

Qualities of a Man

The man that is truly a man,
He has the greatest personality.
His life governed by a gentle hand.
It shines with awesome ability.

Father God Your mercy and peace,
Are qualities he longs for?
Understanding and wisdom against the beast,
Is what he prays.

He is constantly seeking Your guidance,
To help him continue to be meek and humble,
His heart is a mirror of his unshakable stance,
Faithful even after that foreboding stumble.

He praises God without waiver.
In his weakest hour of self control,
He reaches out for strength from the Savior,
Knowing his patience is his goal.

Even to the final hour,
He praises You Father God.
Knowing he is nothing without Your Power,
He praises You Father God.

Life In A Bottle

You say there's a time for a season.
You also say Your hour is to our day.
Dear Lord, what's the reason,
For Your judgment delay?

Is man so lost?
That the mere thought,
Of what it will cost,
He refuses what Your Son has bought.

Sands of the hourglass,
Sieve away the hours.
Man's hope for forgiveness seems to pass,
The Lord's judgment empowers.

There's a time to live life to its fullest,
A time to die.
Is living a way to view which of us is the cruelest,
Is it our way of believing the lie?

I believe we are here to see,
Who can show love among our human race?
Who can hate Thee?
To earn or lose our heavenly place.

Beware!

There's evil lurking everywhere,
Tempting and cursing the human race.
Dying to take us unaware,
They trick us to our face.

A package delivered with pretty designs,
In hopes that you're foolish,
To accept the lies and not the signs,
Served on an unholy dish.

The plan is to take as many souls,
They can before the final hour.
Lies that can surely destroy ones goals,
With deceit of worldly power.

Don't let these monsters destroy your soul.
Beware of your every thought,
They cannot read your thoughts, God has told
Unless you choose, the lies brought.

Choices

I would like to share a thought,
With you today,
It's very important that you have sought,
The Lord and found your way.

Please don't delay!
No one knows the final hour,
So if you foolishly squander your day,
You will lose any or all of your spiritual power.

Fools use their time to play,
As though there was no tomorrow.
The wise use their time to prepare a way,
There will be a tomorrow.

Are you a fool?
Are you the wise man, my friend?
If you choose to be God's tool,
You'll have a glorious end!

Twyla Hickman

Loneliness

Loneliness is like an empty hole.
A place to fill,
It never seems whole.
Never seems real.

Today, I realized I'm alone.
I'm part of a family,
Really, I'm not.
I'm a part of---but not of a family.

I do my part as needed.
Whatever it is and as I am told,
I don't have a choice.
I'm a part of---but not of a family.

I know I'm useful.
I'm not a partner,
I don't have equal rights.
I'm a part of---but not of a family.

I pray Dear God please take me.
Cause giving all I have!
I have nothing that's mine.
I'm a part of – but not of – a family.

The Lord Is Always There

Look into my heart, Dear God!
Help me please the people I love.
I'm so tired God.
I wish I were there with you above.

My soul is so lonely.
It seems so empty.
Ever minute filled with time only,
Hours filled by self-pity.

How do I go on with these pains?
I just want love and understanding.
Have I inherited all of this through my veins?
Is this the result of some evil planning?

It's late and the clock is ticking.
I'm alone – but wait.
I hear something.
It's the Lord; He's never late.

Twyla Hickman
134

Life's Crazy Sayings

Life is full of crazy sayings.
Some are funny.
Some are down right stupid,
For instance-I've written a few.

Too much of something isn't good.
Too little of nothing is bad.
Save your money for a rainy day.
A watched pot never boils.

He's so stubborn,
He'd argue with a stop sign.
He's so tight, he squeaks.
He's so ugly, the dog won't play with him.

If you wash your car, it will rain.
If you have an itch, scratch it.
If you play with frogs, you'll get warts.
If you live in a glass house, don't throw stones.

It's better having a bird in the bush than two in the air.
The early bird gets the worm.
He's as wise as an owl.
Don't count your chickens before they hatch.

These can really tickle.
She really has a bee in her bonnet.
First one smelt it, dealt it.
He's quieter than a church mouse.

Too Many Don'ts

Don't walk in front of a speeding car.
Don't walk under an open ladder.
Don't walk down a dark alley.
Don't walk out of a flying plane.

Don't talk until spoken to.
Don't talk behind someone's back.
Don't talk to strangers.
Don't talk with a mouth full.

Don't leave your clothes in the middle of the floor.
Don't leave food on your plate.
Don't go to the grocery store on an empty stomach.
Don't go too far.

Don't call anyone stupid.
Don't speak until spoken to.
Don't say it if you don't mean it.
Don't cry over spilt milk.

Don't stare at anyone.
Don't drink after someone.
Don't look a gift horse in the mouth.
Don't eat with your fingers.

Don't let the sun set with your anger.
Don't bet on a dead horse.
Don't sleep under a coconut tree.
Don't weep I'm through.

What Part Of It?

Is a house a home?
If there is a family present,
Or is it just a place?
That has four walls to face.

Is a group a family?
If they live together,
Is it simply a group of faces?
Of blood related races.

Is a town a village?
If the houses are close,
Is it just a collection?
Are they gathered for protection?

Are towns what make a country?
If they belong to that land,
Or is it just by fate,
They came to be in that state.

If You Could Walk In His Shoes

Life's expressions have many meanings.
For instance, "If you could walk in his shoes,
Where do they get their beginnings?
Who keeps them in the news?

The first time hearing this,
One wanders why a person would want to.
Surely, this is a misunderstanding to this.
If you could what would you do?

Having even wished at times,
Having been in many places,
Wishing for a couple of dimes,
To have a choice from all these faces.

To walk in someones shoes,
Is not easy to do,
If it is hard for one to choose,
Maybe it is easy for you.

I never want to walk like you.
Knowing it would be hard for me.
But not for you,
Thank God we're different you and me.

Twyla Hickman

That's Not My Job

People often say,
That is not my job.
Often, they get their own way.
It just makes you want to sob.

Wondering what they would say.
If God would say, "it is not my job".
To forgive you today,
Would it make them sob?

Thinking it's everyone's job everyday.
Through life's many ups and downs,
To help each other in every way,
Even if we feel like clowns.

To help when times are gray or lonely,
To help give hope,
Even if it fulfills ones dreams only,
To help them with life's woes to cope.

They will have a job.
To help recruit others,
To keep others from beginning to sob,
With hope for our brothers.

People Of Many Nations

People of many nations,
Have come to see the altar.
Where God was, rejected,
A God for many nations.

More than Himself,
They say He loved everyone.
From His birth to His death,
His life was a testimony of this.

His father asked who would take the stand.
For the sins of man,
Michael the archangel stood up,
Accepted that place before the throne.

Satan angered and enraged with this thought,
Went to earth looking for people of many nations,
That he could deceive,
With his evil tricks and words.

Out of these many nations,
Comes people with different choices,
To stand for God or Satan,
These people of many nations.

Twyla Hickman
140

Windows To The World

Our eyes are windows.
Letting us see the awesomeness of God.
Our hearts are the frames.
That keeps us close to God

Smelling seeing, hearing, tasting, feeling,
These senses are given to us by God.
It is a wondrous thing,
To be able to use your senses, to help others, lost in the fog.

Once there was this precious child.
Calling out for help in a storm,
Thanks to an awesome God,
The child was safe again, in her mothers arms.

That Should Count

Call me crazy.
Nevertheless, didn't you say?
You would love me forever.
That should count.

You always seem happy.
You always say I love you.
You always look like the luckiest man.
That should count.

We were sure of each other.
We promised forever.
Our love always,
That should count.

The days pass by.
The years ease by.
Our love is forever.
That should count.

Everyone and Everything

Everyone has had something lost.
Everyone has something left behind.
Everyone has something to choose.
Everyone has something that was lost or found.

Thinking each day of everything and everyone,
No words to say you are the only one.
You are lost in my memory as one.
You are in the dreams that we are one.

Everyone has problems and troubles.
Everything seems at its worst when it is us who has the pain.
Everyone tries to catch that brass ring.
Everyone lives like there's no tomorrow.

God's Plan

Do you think it is God's, plan,
That the two of you are united?
Will God bless the twosome?
Will God bless your future?

A day to give,
A day to take,
Who will give?
Who will take?

Do you have someone?
Do they have someone?
Are they for you?
Are you for them?

These are simple questions.
While the answers are awesome,
God is in fact all knowing.
So for these answers, Bow your head and listen.

Don't Cry Baby

I cannot remember.
The last time,
You said, "Do not cry baby.
Every thing will be all right.

I woke up one night.
I thought everything,
Had gone away,
You were not there.

I prayed for the day.
To come when you will see,
It is time to change things.
It is changing one's life.

A change for me and for you,
A hope for the future,
A cry for tomorrow,
A prayer for a lifetime.

If These Old Walls Could Talk

You have heard the expression,
If these old walls could talk of tales,
Of what their visitors left on their impression,
They would surely tell some tales.

I once had that pleasure.
I was on a road trip to Big Ben.
I needed a place for a little leisure.
I pulled into a little quaint inn.

I got a key to the room three thirty one red.
I had no idea it was a warning.
I put my pj's on and climbed into bed.
I watched TV until the wee morning.

Began the experience in room 331,
The voices were very clear.
Cannot say I ever saw anyone.
A woman requested a drink, a beer.

I laughed and told her no.
She laughed and said you better.
Because you will have to go,
At that moment, the wall seemed to shudder.

Another voice came from the back of my bed.
"Lady, she thinks she owns the place.
I have tried to sober her up that Miss Red,
She just laughed in my face.

I finally had enough.
I needed to get some sleep tonight.
I said kind of rough,
I really cannot, tonight.

Yes, the walls were polite.
They said they understood.
They got very quite.
That was good.

It is just a thought, my friend.
I think people really do not care.
To hear a wall talk now and then,
Even though it is very rare.

We've Come Into The Twenty First Century

We have purchased a state of the art computer, wow.
We have come into the twenty first century, too.
Through pinching pennies that is how,
We got a computer brand new.

Shortly after the New Year,
We got our baby home.
We thought we would simply bust a gear,
Games for him and writing for me at home.

Waited and waited and waited,
Patiently for my turn,
My husband needed to check it out he stated.
After three weeks, I began to burn.

We had to sit down,
To make a schedule for our baby,
I could play with it anytime he was out of town,
Except when he is in town maybe.

He Stands

He stands as a boy in a man's body.
He stands tall to fight the world's game.
He stands against all the world's odds.
He stands this worldly man.

He stands to try to fight for his place in this world.
He stands to show the world his worth.
He stands to show his children his love.
He stands to show his strength in knowledge of his love.

Sweet prince, you're just a man.
One created for just that task.
God loves you-you are in his image.
He wants you to stand tall against the world's foes.

He knows you kneel before Him.
You praise His wisdom and ask for His guidance.
He stands tall with your decisions.
You're made with Him in mind.

Man and Woman

Many years ago,
He walked into her life.
Not even in her eyes,
He did not look like much.

He walked, he prayed.
He worshipped, he hoped,
That some day,
That certain someone would appear.

Then one day he looked up,
There she stood.
An angel in his eyes,
Her body was that of perfection.

Her voice was soft and sweet.
Her hopes were strong.
Her prayers were hopeful to his ears.
Her spirit was strong and constant.

She tried to change herself.
Her prayers were for guidance,
Heard by the Savior,
He blessed her with a gift of His grace.

Questions

Have you ever wondered?
If God gets tired,
The Bible says.
He is from infinity to infinity.

Is it just my weak mind?
Which cannot fathom His Greatness?
Is it just my imperfection?
Given to me by my ancestors.

Is it the end of life?
Is the beginning the end?
Is it a dream?
Is it a reflection of life?

Does God really exist?
Is He our hope for a future?
Does Satan exist?
Is he merely a reason for our failures?

The Shortest Sentence

The shortest sentence,
Do you know what it is?
It is not the punishment.
It is the statement.

It is in the Bible.
The book of God,
It is not deniable.
It is from a follower of God.

He cried.
Jesus did this too.
He did not hide.
He showed the world, He felt grief, too.

He wanted the world to see,
That we were to have great compassion,
For ourselves and for you and me,
This was His gift – compassion.

He said to love one another.
Not just your friends,
Your enemies as your brother,
Love your father and mother to the very end my friends.

A Friend's Betrayal

A friend that betrays you,
Is worse than an open wound.
It will not heal,
Thus, like an enemy's wound.

You can only hope,
That your friend cares for you,
Like you care for them,
Hope, trust, and honor.

One can trust himself.
But to trust another,
It is the greatest tie that binds.
That will endure with time.

Do you know your enemy?
From your friend,
One could say there is a thin line,
That divides them.

Every time you reach out,
Your hand is the one bitten.
Only teaches you one thing,
You should be writing it on your heart.

Choose your friends wisely.
Decide who you want to be yours.
And who you despise,
You can keep them from entering your doors.

You Are A Lady

I met a girl today.
I should say she was a lady,
In a proper way,
Her eyes lit up when she spoke.

Her tiny and delicate frame,
Supported a tender and loving heart,
Her smile is reassuring.
She had every thing in control.

There is a hint of concern,
Behind the words of comfort,
Her words are very uplifting.
They fill you with awe for her.

She is simple yet intriguing.
She is quiet yet outgoing.
She is meek yet forceful if need be.
She is honest yet able to listen.

Dear God, I want to be like her.
If this is in Your master plan,
Give me the strength and guidance.
I will pursue this in all my trials in life.

Twyla Hickman
154

It Is Better

Is it better to be right?
Than to be justified,
Is it better to be happy
Than to be sad?

Is it better to be safe?
Than to be wild
Is it better to be alive
Than to be dead?

Is it better to be sure?
Than to be sorry
Is it better to have a family
Than to be alone?

Is it better to surrender?
Than to fight
Is it better to be strong
Than to be weak?

Is it better to be an optimist?
Than to be a pessimist
Than to be awake
Than to be asleep?

Is it better to be rich?
Than to be poor
Is it better to be bright
Than it is to be dull?

Is it better to be first?
Than it is to be last
Is it better to be thin
Than it is to be fat?

Is it better to be healthy?
Than it is to be sick
Is it better to be a writer,
Than it is to be reader?

Rage

I have known some rages.
They have known me.
I have tasted them at several ages.
So bitter, I could not see.

If you can conquer the rages,
Of your life's worth,
Written in the history pages,
Of time since your birth.

Rages of man or woman,
Tells one how they view their worth.
Rage out of control will destroy a man.
It starts with ones birth.

How Will The World End?

There are several thoughts going around about it.
A couple of them are.
That fire will consume the world,
Or maybe ice.

It is sure to think fire.
One tastes it every time he lies.
Desire is a taste of fire.
A simple kiss gives thoughts of fires.

On the other hand, is it ice?
One tastes it every time he hates.
The cold shoulder carries a price.
Perishing with hate sealing our fates.

Life As Seen By A Child

A young child sees life,
As a wonderful and beautiful place,
Sometimes the child wants life,
To be a magical and miraculous place.

Dreams turn the child in us,
To be completely happy, joyful and even grateful,
Dreaming in our youth helps to trust,
It seems this is only temporary.

It is the child in us,
That helps us to continue to hope, dream, and grow,
In God we must trust.
No one else.

Twyla Hickman

Do You Ever Think?

Do you ever think?
It's my time not yours.
Do you ever hope?
This day is mine.

I know this may be,
Hard to believe,
I know this may seem,
Crazy and not real.

I was thinking about life.
As the way it continues.
It is not always,
The way it should be.

Just as I find out,
The reason for the questions,
Then just as life is clear,
The answers are not clear now!

Did You Think?

Did you think?
I was leaving again.
Did you say?
That is all right.
We can be friends.

Did you throw my things out?
It hurt like a knife in the back.
Did you try to get along?
With anyone and everyone,
Jesus and his apostles did.

They say the proof is in the pudding.
My love, I try to understand.
I love you without a catch.
My love is yours forever.
My dreams are of you.

My hope for the future,
Is in your hands.

Twyla Hickman

Patchwork Quilt

When I was strong,
Foolish and headstrong,
I took for granted.
She would always be there.

Running from school to home,
Smelling her homemade cooking,
I remember lying on the cold tile floor.
Underneath the quilt, being hand stitched.

Hours quickly flew by,
When there was a quilting bee.
Quilts made from dresses and pants,
Some from a bride or family member.

Patchwork quilts cherished.
They bring to mind times,
Filled with joy and laughter,
Even times of hardship perhaps even disaster.

One's Lonely Hour

You can feel the absence,
In this ones lonely hour,
Without any kind of sense,
Of all that matters, grows sour.

You can look in the faces,
Of those who want to be.
More than those in lower places,
Only stay close to the potter's knee.

The waiting, comes and goes.
The hoping stays constant.
A man knows his difficulties from any other Joe's.
God makes one soul soar to a greater constant.

Praying with great hope for the power,
In ones last hour,
To be taken home,
A place of comfort, a place to call home

Man's Fulfilment

Now it is the fulfillment of life.
You have asked, would you take a wife.
You have fulfilled his dream.
His life is complete it would seem.

Never a dream to come true,
He thinks each day of you.
No words to say, you are the one.
In his memory of you, there is no other one.

You will let the dream fill his head.
He is complete without dread.
You fulfill his dreams.
Forever he smiles with great joy it seems.

A dream is something that one sees.
If the dream is to help you with your needs,
Life is the road we take,
Or it is what we make.

Man and Angels

To look into one's soul,
To see what others see,
Hoping to reach one's goal,
Hoping to be all one can be,

Walk the straight and narrow path.
Trying to save ones' soul,
That takes strength and faith,
To reach our heavenly goal.

Angels stand by us watching.
They are pure and innocent in form.
Angels help us fight evil's testing.
They give us strength against all harm.

Twyla Hickman
164

My World And All That I See

My world and all that I see,
My husband and my children,
My family and acquaintances,
My friends and even my enemies,

Every occasion is a time to reflect.
On who has changed and who has not.
On the good times and the bad,
On how many more will one have.

Every birth is a season to rejoice.
And every death, too,
We are happy at a new life,
Sad at the end of one.

There are difficulties in life.
We are taught, we must take the good with the bad.
Not dwell on the hard times,
Look to the good times.

As for my world and all that I see,
I count my blessing.
Thank God for every moment in it.
Life's short enough without any guessing.